Developing a Strategic Plan for Your Business

A Step by Step Guide to Strategic Planning

By Meir Liraz

(Including 10 Special Bonuses)

Published by Liraz Publishing

www.BizMove.com

Copyright © Liraz Publishing. All rights reserved.

ISBN: 9781695382701

Table of Contents

1. introduction — 5
2. The Need For a Strategic Plan — 9
3. Creating a Mission Statement — 13
4. Defining Your Business — 15
5. Setting Your Firm's Goals — 17
6. Environmental and Industry Analysis — 23
7. Internal Business Analysis — 17
8. Finalizing The Plan — 32
9. Implementing The Strategy — 37
10. Summary — 43

Supplements:

11. A System For Applying The Strategic Plan in Your Business — 46
12. Creating a Business Environment that Supports Growth — 61
13. How to Ensure That Your Business is On The Right Path — 80
Appendix: Special Free Bonuses — 97

MEIR LIRAZ

1. Introduction

To many people, strategic planning is something meant only for big businesses, but it is equally applicable to small businesses. Strategic planning is matching the strengths of your business to available opportunities. To do this effectively, you need to collect, screen and analyze information about the business environment. You also need to have a clear understanding of your business - its strengths and weaknesses - and develop a clear mission, goals and objectives. Acquiring this understanding often involves more work than expected. You must realistically assess the business you are convinced you know well. Familiarity can breed contempt for thorough analysis; you cannot properly evaluate your firm's strengths or shortcomings.

The Business Environment

Strategic planning focuses largely on managing interaction with environmental forces, which include competitors, government, suppliers, customers, various interest groups and other factors that affect your business and its prospects. Your ability as a small business owner-manager to deal with these groups will vary widely depending on the group and on the timing. Also, you may be able to get more of what you want from a supplier than from a competitor (although size, distance, the percentage of the supplier's business you represent and your record of dependability as a customer can affect this relationship). How you manage these and other relationships is one of the decisions you will make during the strategic planning process.

Because of major changes in the business environment, your familiarity with strategic planning and your ability to implement it is critical. At one time, business owner-managers assessed the environment on a continuum that ran between very stable and very unstable. Businesses, such as the producers of automobiles, furniture and other consumer goods, operated in a relatively stable and predictable world. This also was true of many service firms, such as banks and savings and loans. Typically, the environment included competition that was limited to a stable group of competitors, loyal customers and a relatively slow transfer of information. Many small businesses could thrive in this environment. Other small investors entered fields such as xerography, computers and computer component production, software design and chemical research. Some of these grew rapidly, becoming names with which we all are familiar: Xerox, IBM, Apple and Microsoft. But many more failed.

Today, experts agree that more businesses face an unstable business environment. Improvements in information processing and telecommunications have made major changes in most industries. Along with this, improvements in transportation and the growth of foreign economies (specifically in Europe and Asia) have created a global marketplace and redefined certain industries. In addition, as consumers are exposed to more choices, loyalty has become less important than it once was; a slightly better deal or a temporary shortage of stock can easily result in the loss of customers. Competitors also can change rapidly, with new ones appearing from out of nowhere (often this means the other side of the globe). With the instability of the global market, it is important that you make strategic planning part of your overall business strategy.

Proactive Versus Reactive Management

A few years ago, you could establish and maintain a business by reacting to and meeting changes in tastes, costs and prices. This reactive style of management was often enough to keep the business going. However, today changes happen fast and come from many directions. By the time a reactive manager can make the necessary adjustments, he or she may lose many customers -- possibly for good.

Proactive planning is the anticipation of future events. Decisions are based on predictions of future states of the environment as opposed to reactions to various crises as they occur. Proactive planning in an unstable, technology-driven business environment is critical to continuing success in almost any endeavor. Rather than reacting to the situation as it changes, proactive planning requires that you analyze environmental forces and make resource-allocation decisions. By doing this you will take your business where it needs to be in the next month, year and decade. Barry Worth, a consultant specializing in small business management, puts it this way: Today's entrepreneur must be a business architect. Anything built in today's business environment must have a step-by-step blueprint or plan on how to achieve success.

The blueprint for today's business owner is a business plan.

2. The Need for a Strategic Plan

Planning plays an important role in any business venture. It can make the difference between the success or failure of your business. You should plan carefully before investing your time and, especially, your money in any business venture. The need for a plan is best illustrated by the following scenario - "A Tale of Two Businesses."

Two franchises (A and B) were started by individuals who had worked in management in much larger companies. While Franchise A provided a product and Franchise B a service, the output of both franchise systems had been sold exclusively in the United States before the current owners became involved. The output of both was readily available in other developed countries as well. The franchises opened about the same time and neither franchisee had a strong market presence, nor do they at present. Today Franchise B is bankrupt. By contrast, Franchise A is selling products in the Midwestern United States and in Europe.

What was the deciding difference in the two franchises' success? You probably expect it to be that one had developed a strategic plan and the other hadn't; however, it isn't this simple. Many factors can influence the outcome of a business venture. There were many similarities between the franchises, but there also were many differences.

Most notably, Franchise A sold a product and Franchise B a service (although this does not clearly limit options). Another difference was that Franchise A had a carefully thought-out plan. The investors knew as they looked for a franchise partner that they wanted to find a product that could satisfy international markets and a franchiser who would support that kind of sales effort. These investors were based in the Midwest, but negotiated for exclusive rights to export the franchiser's product. Once they had obtained the franchise, and as they began to establish their business domestically, they also began to contact government experts in the U.S. Department of Commerce as well as educators and local managers with international experience.

Clear plans were developed outlining how they would position, market and distribute the product and which foreign markets would be targeted first. Even as they were building sales in one European market, they were attending trade shows and planning entry strategies in others.

By contrast, the second investor (Franchise B) started his business strictly because he wanted to leave a former employer. Of course many small businesses get started this way; however, in this case

DEVELOPING A STRATEGIC PLAN

no investigation of franchising alternatives was done. The business was located in an area that, as it turned out, contained virtually no consumers for the kind of service being offered. When this mistake was realized, it was too late to move--the investor simply did not have the money or the desire to risk starting again.

Other examples further show the need for strategic planning and for developing a clear business plan. The owner of a business that seemed to be doing quite well in two locations was about to open in a third. The authors were called in to develop a benefits policy and discovered cash flow problems that could be found only after operations had begun in the new location. After analyzing the situation, an expansion and financial plan was developed for the sound locations only. In another case, the authors determined that a business had purchased more equipment than was necessary to accomplish the current workload.

After careful analysis, plans to make further purchases were put on hold, and the equipment available was used effectively to meet immediate needs.

A business enterprise is to complex to assume that failure to develop a sound business plan will be the cause for problems Nevertheless, this failure often counts among the factors contributing to business difficulties. As Worth has said, "Being a business entrepreneur today takes constant vigilance in order to be able to take advantage of new opportunities and the availability of new information and technology as they come into being." The first step in doing this is to have a plan.

3. Creating a Mission Statement

The first step in the strategic planning process is an assessment of the market. Businesses depend on consumers for their existence. If you are facing a rapidly growing consumer base, you probably will plan differently than if your clientele is stable or shrinking. If you are lucky enough to be in a business where brand loyalty still prevails, you may take risks that others cannot afford to take. Before you begin to assess the market, it is important that you complete a careful assessment of your own business and its goals.

The outcome of this self-assessment process is known as the mission statement. According to Glueck and Jauch, "The mission can be seen as a link between performing some social function and the more specific targets or objectives of the organization." Another definition states that the mission statement is a "term that refers to identifying an organization's current and future business. It is viewed as the primary objective of the organization".

Because these authors are writing for an audience of managers or would-be managers of larger businesses, their definitions may sound a bit lofty. If, however, you go back to the earlier example of a successful small business, you can see it started with a clear direction--what was to be achieved and, in a broad sense, how best to achieve it. While your own goal may be to survive, make a profit, be your own boss or even be rich, your business must first perform a social function, i.e., I must serve someone. Given this you must determine (1) the ultimate purpose and (2) the specific targets or objectives of your business.

The investors of Franchise A discussed above clearly had determined they wanted a business with the potential for international sales. With this objective they were able to determine the kind of franchise they wanted and the terms. They knew that some goods and services were more likely to be marketable overseas than others. Early research helped them determine which areas of the world would be the best places to start. This, in turn, helped them to further narrow their list of potential products. Also, they were able to assess the financial demands of various approaches to overseas markets. Their financial analysis enabled them to affirm that a franchise would be one of the alternatives with a high profit potential. All of these directions were derived from an initially vague desire to "go international." And, as the investors developed their ideas into a clearly defined business purpose, many issues were discovered that were critical to success.

4. Defining Your Business

A primary concern in defining a mission statement is addressing the question "What business are you in?" Answering this may seem fairly easy; however, it can be a complex task. Determining the nature of your business should not be strictly tied to the specific product or service you currently produce. Rather, it must be tied to the result of your output--your social function--and the competencies you have developed in producing that output.

Management theorist Peter Drucker suggests that if the railroad companies of the early 1900s or the wagonmakers of the 1800s had defined their business purpose as that of developing a firm position in the transportation business, rather than limiting themselves strictly to the rail or wagon business, they might still enjoy the market positions they once did. The obvious concern here is to ensure that you do not define your business too narrowly, leaving yourself open to economic changes or competitive challenges that make you vulnerable. The primary reason the service company mentioned earlier (Franchise B) failed was that it lacked a consumer base. These consumers were already being served by the current market. In another example, an entrepreneur developed a device to provide greater security for homes and vehicles. But, by focusing on the product rather than the service it was meant to provide, he failed to consider other services that already provided essentially the same level of protection at lower costs.

Your Firm's Philosophy

Once you have defined your mission statement, the next step is to define the firm's basic philosophy. Such a statement will help explain to your employees and associates how you would like to see the firm operate. Are you a risk taker, or would you prefer to build your business slowly from a solid base? How will you relate to customers, suppliers and competitors? What type of community involvement do you plan for your business, e.g., participation in recycling and volunteer activities? These questions, and many more, need clear answers to help your employees make operational decisions and conduct themselves in a manner consistent with your wishes. Much has been written about this concept in business literature under the term corporate culture. A clear explanation of your business's philosophy in the mission statement will provide a basis for the development of a consistent business culture.

DEVELOPING A STRATEGIC PLAN

5. Setting Your Firm's Goals

The next step is to set clear goals to guide and maintain the business on a path consistent with its mission. Daniel Robey provides an excellent list of the key functions of business goals. To summarize his comments, goals serve to:

Justify or legitimize the organization's activities.

Focus attention and set constraints for member behavior.

Identify the nature of the organization and elicit commitment.

Reduce uncertainty by clarifying what the organization is pursuing.

Help an organization to learn and adapt by showing discrepancies between goals and actual progress (providing feedback).

Serve as a standard of assessment for organization members.

Provide a rationale for organization design.

At one time, it was widely assumed that the owner of a company set that firm's goals. Glueck and Jauch refer to this as a "trickled-own" theory because it was assumed that others in the organization simply accepted these goals. Chester Barnard, believing that it was naive to assume such ready acceptance, suggested that organizational objectives arose from a consensus of the employees. This "trickle-up" theory, however, is also naive in assuming that an organization is simply the sum of individual perspectives, and that it can achieve direction from an unguided and usually disparate group of people. Modern theories spring from combinations of these two approaches, suggesting goal development is a complex goal-bargaining process that enjoys some advantages of both basic theories.

Bargaining, while seeming a rather negative and poorly developed goal-setting approach, has the advantage of involving most, if not all, employees in the process. As a result, it is more likely that key concerns, internal as well as external, will be taken into account. By involving employees, you improve their understanding of and commitment to the firm.

Pierce and Robinson captured the complexity of goal setting in this statement: Strategic choice is the simultaneous selection of long-range objectives and grand strategy.... When strategic planners study their opportunities, they try to determine which are most likely to result in achieving various long-range objectives. Almost simultaneously, they try to forecast whether an available grand strategy can take advantage of preferred opportunities so that the tentative objectives can be met. In essence then, three distinct but highly interdependent choices are being made at one time. Usually several triads or sets of possible decisions are considered.

To improve the structure of this strategic approach, most experts suggest that a repetitive method be used in developing goals. This begins with the owner and perhaps a few key employees agreeing on a long-term direction for the business and suggesting major goals in line with this direction. Then, other employees are asked to suggest specific objectives, which are then reviewed before being implemented. Goals become the shared purposes of the owner and employees and thus, it is much easier to get the support of employees and their clear understanding of what needs to be accomplished.

Goals are defined as broad, ideal conditions. A possible goal could be "To become the leading small-package delivery service in the Kansas City metropolitan area." In defining goals it is important to understand (1) how the goal was derived and (2) how it provides guidance.

Objectives to Achieve Goals

Accomplishing a goal requires establishing and achieving several specific objectives, which must

Be clear, concise and attainable.

Be measurable.

Have a target date for completion.

Include responsibility for taking action.

Be arranged according to priority.

An objective to the above-stated goal could require that the dispatcher develop a route structure capable of providing three-hour service to any area within 20 miles of the city's center, with the service beginning within six months.

An objective has to fit within a hierarchical network of other objectives that together contribute to the firm's ultimate goals and mission. For example, a subsidiary objective to the one mentioned above may be "To purchase three new or late-model used delivery vans within five months." Another objective could specify expanding staff to drive the additional vehicles and to handle the expected increase in dispatching chores. This system of setting priorities is called a hierarchy of objectives.

Anthony Raia provides a list of guidelines to help you avoid pitfalls in setting objectives. Some of the most important include:

Adapt your objectives directly to organizational

goals and strategic plans. Do not assume that they support higher level management objectives.

Quantify and target the results whenever possible. Do not formulate objectives where attainment cannot be measured or at least verified.

Test your objectives for challenge and achievability. Do not build in cushions to hedge against accountability for results.

Adjust the objectives to the available resources and the realities of organizational life. Do not keep your head either in the clouds or in the sand.

Establish performance reports and milestones that measure progress toward the objective. Do not rely on instinct or crude benchmarks to appraise performance.

Put your objectives in writing and express them in clear, concise and unambiguous statements. Do not allow them to remain in loose or vague terms.

Limit the number of statements of objectives to the key result areas (for your business). Do not obscure priorities by slating too many objectives.

Review your statements with others to assure

consistency and mutual support. Do not fall into the trap of setting your objectives in a vacuum.

Modify your statements to meet changing conditions and priorities.

Do not continue to pursue objectives that have become obsolete.

The formulation of a mission, goals and objectives is a complex, repetitive and continual process. As a small business owner-manager, your first reaction may be that you don't have the time or the resources to accomplish this. This may be true; however, you must develop a process that you can implement and be comfortable with. You will need to be aware of this process, the relationship of goals to ultimate performance and the need to be specific and consistent. A carefully throughout set of goals provides the base on which the rest of strategic planning will proceed. The time you put into carefully assessing what you hope to achieve and how you will measure it will reduce the time required to assess and control performance.

6. Environmental and Industry Analysis

In determining appropriate goals, you will need to consider the position of your business within its industry and the broader business environment. Several trends may affect your business prospects. Examples may include shifts in population (e.g., the purchasing status of "baby boomers"), trends in the economy, technological developments, legislation (e.g., safety or antipollution regulation) and the activities of special interest groups. As you clarify your mission and goals, you will find that some factors are important while others may not require your attention.

There are several approaches to dealing with fluctuation and change in your business environment. James Thompson presents a list of general strategies that provides a good "first cut" at the complicated process of making strategic choices related to the business environment. He argues that most organizations search for certainty in an uncertain, fluctuating environment. Depending on the business' resources and the specific situation, a business may adopt one of four approaches to the business environment.

Buffering can be used when you have an abundance of resources, sometimes referred to as organizational slack. However, this is a luxury few efficiently run businesses enjoy. If, for example, you possess a technological edge, you may be able to relax your vigilance in the confidence that you have the resources to adapt to changes that may occur. You are then able to concentrate on other environmental factors that may affect areas of your business in which you don't have such an advantage.

Smoothing is a useful approach when you enjoy surplus resources in one area but your ability to meet demand is overtaxed in others. A good example is a chimney cleaning service that was unable to meet demands for chimney repair and service during the winter months, but had to lay off employees during the spring and summer months. In an attempt to change the environment, the owner developed advertising and pricing strategies aimed at attracting more business during slow times. In addition the owner assessed the skills of his employees. He found that by doing general masonry jobs in slow times, he could retain workers while actually increasing the size of his business. This example also provides a clear illustration of how a small business can manage, and even change, its environment.

Forecasting is something, that all businesses must do. When you don't have the resources to use a buffering strategy or when conditions make smoothing impossible, you must anticipate environmental changes. The immediate need of most businesses is to monitor the competition. Other events that you can anticipate with an effective forecasting system include:

Technological breakthroughs.

New competitors (either a company "purchases in to" your industry or a new competitor enters from an overseas market).

Changes in the cost and availability of raw materials.

Changes in consumer taste.

Effective forecasting is possible only when probabilities can be predicted; for example, you have a pretty good idea of what the odds are that shortages will occur in a raw material, or what the chances are that a law will pass providing new sources of assistance to small businesses. Unfortunately, many trends and changes are very difficult, if not impossible, to anticipate, even with the best forecasting system.

As a result you may find that you must resort to Thompson's fourth approach - rationing. An unanticipated technological breakthrough or a sudden change in the spending habits of your customers may force you to reallocate resources. In this situation, goals may need to be delayed or foregone altogether, and parts of your business may need to be reduced. All needs of the business will not be completely met, but you will move to a base from which you will have the best chance to recover. With time you will rebuild to compensate for any losses incurred.

Information Needs

The most important consideration in developing an effective approach to forecasting and planning is the development of your information system. In the world of personal computers, you may equate information systems with microchips and programming, but the concept as used here is much broader, referring to the way you gather, screen, analyze and use information that may affect your business. This guide is part of your information system. You are using it to inform yourself of modern approaches to managing, improving and possibly enlarging your business.

Too many businesses still have information systems that might be described as "shoe-box" systems. Information about the business and its environment are collected in various documents that are stored in shoe boxes, or it is picked up through contacts between the owner and customers. The owner "analyzes" this information and the results are used to make further decisions.

The problems with this system are obvious. First, no effort has been made to determine what critical elements--internal or external to the business--should be assessed. Second, assessment is based entirely on what strikes the owner as memorable or important. Unfortunately, what is remembered is not necessarily what is important. Memory is influenced by preconceptions and perceptions, and by how busy, tired or distracted the owner was at the time an event occurred. An additional problem with this informal approach is that, should the owner want to verify his or her impressions of some series of events, it would be time consuming-- if not impossible--to locate the records that would allow a full analysis. While "seat-of-the-pants" decision making based on this type of information system sometimes works remarkably well, much is left to chance.

Setting up an effective information system is integrally related to your mission and goals and to the specific environmental factors defined in your strategic purpose. Collect enough information, but don't collect too much-- this leads to information overload, where decision makers are so swamped they become incapable of making sense of the information, or of using it to make good decisions.

Developing a good system is a dynamic process. It is easy to determine what information you need to collect and how to obtain it. However, as the environment and your situation change, the information you need also changes. Items that were once important now are not. Other considerations, impossible to anticipate at the time you developed your system, have become critical.

Employees should be involved in determining what information is needed and where to obtain it. They are often the first line for data collection. They can provide insights and perspectives that you may not have considered. Together, you will be able to develop a reasonably thorough list of concerns that the information system should address.

In any information system, a variety of sources should always be used. You already collect much information in the documents you use to conduct everyday business. Other sources may include periodicals (particularly those published specifically for your industry), newspapers (or clipping services), books and experts in areas of concern.

Once you have collected the data, you will need to condense and analyze it. This is the information reporting system. You already produce reports for various government agencies and banks, which are nothing more than a presentation of the data you collect in a way that is useful to the particular agency. A good information system will provide information to employees in your business in a form that they need to make effective decisions and carry out their jobs. It will provide enough information, but not more than is necessary and useful. As the type of data collected changes over time, so will the reports needed. As a result, report requirements must be periodically reassessed so time is not spent producing useless reports.

Finally, information should be stored for easy retrieval to accommodate new situations that may require different analyses. In data processing, this system of storage is referred to as the company's data base. Whether you rely on an electronic or a manual system, storing information so it is easily retrievable requires considerable forethought. Much of the business software available today focuses on storing data in ways that allow it to be retrieved in many different forms and later combined for analyses that were not originally anticipated or necessary.

7. Internal Business Analysis

Once you've begun to collect the necessary information about your external environment, you will be able to consider how to best fit your business into the situations that surface. To do this you must clearly understand the strengths and weaknesses of your firm. For a long time, people assumed that small businesses were always at a disadvantage because they were small. Today, there are few commercial areas that don't have room for smaller competitors if they are focused and efficient.

The primary task in the business analysis phase is to identify those factors that may give you a competitive advantage. If you hold a patent or an exclusive license on a particular product or service, you may enjoy a competitive advantage. Flexibility is a major advantage that small businesses often enjoy over larger rivals. You may be able to respond more quickly and with less cost to mood swings or taste changes in the market. Also, small businesses can often move into new product or service lines more quickly than larger firms.

The nature of the technology used to make your product may often yield competitive advantages. If you employ individuals skilled in areas unique to your business, their skills will often yield cost advantages that may offset disadvantages in other areas. For example, your competitor may be further ahead in using computer-aided scheduling, but you are able to rely on specialists in your own firm and can market your product as a unique value while you move to minimize the technological differential. Once you are clear about the areas in which you are ahead, assess your weaknesses. Having done this, you can develop a strategy that has the best chance of succeeding. Instead of simply trying to compete for customers on a single dimension, such as price, or to catch up in one area of technology, you are now able to consider alternatives derived from a combination of factors. You may, for example, see that a traditional competitor has an apparently insurmountable cost advantage from adopting a technology that yielded unforeseen benefits. An effort to compete strictly on the basis of price while attempting to catch up technologically is probably doomed to failure. On the other hand, a move into other product lines that take advantage of the skills used by your firm may give you a better chance for survival. Eventually, this strategy may give you the time needed to acquire the technology to compete in your original product area.

8. Finalizing The Plan

When you have a clear grasp of the competitors, customers, suppliers and situations you face, and you combine this with a realistic understanding of your own strengths and weaknesses, you can develop a strategic plan with a strong chance of success. You may decide that you have the strengths to compete with other businesses "head-to-head" in their best markets. You may choose to target a market that has not been touched by your competitors. You may see opportunities to influence local or state legislation in a way favorable to your needs. Or you may realize that you are constrained by a combination of circumstances that severely restrict your opportunities and leave you only limited chances for success. You should, however, under any of these scenarios, be able to make better choices.

Before you develop a detailed plan to implement, attempt to identify several possible alternative approaches. Frequently, when an individual or organization faces a problem or opportunity, solutions will appear to "pop up." You've faced similar situations before, you have a "gut feeling" that the way to solve the problem is to.... " While your first idea may, in fact, work, the odds are it won't be as effective as other possibilities. The reason that this obvious choice may not be the best option is that it is usually based on experiences that, while appearing similar, are actually very different. You may struggle a bit to identify other possible approaches. No alternative will be perfect. But once you have considered several and listed the advantages, disadvantages and overall chances of success for each alternative, you will be in a better position to settle on a plan with greater potential.

The Business Plan

The business plan is a succinct document that specifies the components of a strategy with regard to the business mission, external and internal environments and problems identified in earlier analyses. A business plan is not written each time a modification to a strategy is made. It should be written when you develop a new venture or launch a major new initiative. The business plan serves several important purposes:

It helps determine the viability of the venture in a designated market.

It provides guidance to the entrepreneur in organizing his or her planning activities.

It serves as an important tool in helping to obtain financing.

A well-written business plan also will provide broad parameters upon which progress toward goals can be assessed and control decisions made at a later time.

A typical business plan begins with a brief introduction followed by an executive summary. The executive summary is prepared after the total plan has been written. Its purpose is to communicate the plan in a convincing way to important audiences, such as potential investors, so they will read further.

An industry analysis usually follows the executive summary. This section communicates key information--the collection of which was discussed earlier--that puts the venture or plan into the proper context.

The marketing plan is the first step in developing any new strategy. It is developed within the context of the company's goals and should be based on a realistic assessment of the external environment, as discussed earlier. The marketing plan is written first because marketing decisions typically determine resource needs in other areas. Obviously, a decision to seek a large share of a market will require a significant commitment of resources of various kinds. How you choose to promote and distribute your product or service will have clear ramifications for your organizational, production, human resource and financial plans.

The organizational plan details how your business is to be configured to most effectively support the marketing objectives. What kinds of skills are needed to carry out your plan? What sorts of skills do you have among managers and employees? What tasks will be done by which employees? What tasks will be contracted out? Many businesses, for example, hire the services of an advertising firm to improve their product promotions but handle their customer relations internally. Roles and responsibilities of each employee need to be clearly specified, as discussed in the section on goal setting.

Develop the production plan and human resources plan along with the organizational plan. Again, you must decide whether or not you will handle all production internally or contract all or part of it to other firms. What equipment will you need to meet the marketing plan? What will be the costs of manufacturing the product? What will be the future capital needs of the enterprise?

Human resource needs are clearly affected by decisions made in production planning. What human resources do you have? Will they be adequate to handle new or changed plans? What additional skills are needed? Will you seek employees who are already trained, or will you hire less skilled individuals and train them? If the latter, what resources will be needed for training, and how long will it take to obtain the desired levels of productivity?

The financial plan underpins this entire system of plans. Three financial areas are generally discussed. First, forecasted sales and related expenses need to be summarized. Monthly figures generally need to be estimated for a period exceeding one year, although the appropriate period will vary depending on the nature of the product and the stability of the market. Second, cash flow figures need to be estimated over the same period. A business needs to pay its bills in a timely fashion; many successful ventures end when suppliers refuse to extend additional credit to a business that hasn't paid its bills. Finally, a projected balance sheet that shows the financial condition of your business at a specific time needs to be prepared.

Usually an appendix is included in a business plan. This generally contains supporting information, documents and details that would interfere with clear communication in the body of the plan. Examples of this type of information include price lists, economic forecasts, demographic data and market analyses.

9. Implementing The Strategy

Implementation is usually thought of as something you do at the end of the strategic planning process. "Okay, now we have this strategic plan; let's do it." If you think about what has been discussed in this guide, it becomes apparent that you will be considering the practical problems of implementation throughout the planning process. Frequently, a suggested alternative will be rejected because it would be difficult to implement. Or a preferred approach to marketing or production would be beyond the financial means of you or your investors.

The two primary issues that need to be considered in the final implementation process are communication and scheduling. Successfully implementing a plan depends on effective communication. Employee resistance often can be reduced, if not eliminated, if plans are openly presented and concerns are dealt with up front. In addition, to carry out new policies and procedures effectively, employees need to have a clear understanding of what is happening and what is expected of them. Better informed employees are more likely to do as you instruct them, thereby reducing the need for complex and costly control systems.

One key element in effective communication is involving your employees--those who must carry out the plan--as much as possible in the actual planning process. People who are involved in planning will have a solid grasp of the plan and their part in it when it is implemented. If employees are genuinely involved in the process, they are more likely to accept the result as a plan they helped develop. This result is often referred to as "ownership."

Successful implementation also depends on a realistic schedule for the transition. It is too easy to assume away the difficulties of a major change and to anticipate that everything will be on track and running smoothly. How many times have you seen a news report about schedule and cost overruns on a government project? This kind of error can be disastrous if you are working within tight margins that can be quickly eradicated when costs and sales don't reach expectations on time. Realistic schedules require that you factor in training time, periods of low productivity, increased error rates and slowdowns as you correct organizational oversights. Schedules also should include planned checkpoints for carefully assessing progress toward full implementation.

Every business needs to develop systems for measuring and controlling progress toward strategic goals; no matter how loyal your employees or how strong the camaraderie, individual and organizational goals are not always the same. Three features distinguish effective control systems from ineffective systems.

Standards -These are your specific operative goals. The need to carefully set clear and measurable goals was emphasized earlier. (The processes of planning and controlling are most closely related for this reason.) Cautiously interpret how well your business performs relative to your goals. It is too easy to assume that, if you are not meeting your goals, the business simply is falling short. You also must reassess your original goals. Are the goals reasonable? Is it possible that you overestimated the firm's capabilities? Has something changed in the environment--a new law, a new competitor, an economic downturn that has completely changed the playing field? If, for whatever reason, your goals are now too high, your employees, if forced to continue to pursue them, will become exasperated rather than motivated.

Measurement - control systems must include quantifiable measures for monitoring performance. The lack of effective measurement systems is where control systems often fail. If you can set performance standards for profits and units produced, if you can tie standards directly to the goals of the plan, then building an effective measurement system is less difficult. Unfortunately, there are many tasks, particularly in management, that are difficult to assess. The output of these tasks, while critical to the overall success of the plan, is not usually measurable in clear units. Payoffs often only come after a long interval.

Corrective measures - corrective actions must be carefully directed at the cause of discrepancies between planned and actual results, and the cause of problems is often very difficult to identify. It is fairly easy, for example, to blame an individual worker for goal failures. However, in complex business systems, where labor and sophisticated technology interact, production systems require careful coordination by managers who must deal with vast amounts of information. In the modern business world, it is becoming harder to identify the source of problems with one agent.

In setting up an effective control system, you need to make five key design decisions:

Will you use behavior or output controls? As noted earlier, output controls are easier to develop if they can be directly related to the goal. Unfortunately, for many jobs, output controls don't make sense because of the indirect link between day-to-day work and long-term output.

Do you have adequate means of measuring progress? Frequently, it is wise to use multiple measures of job and organization performance. Too many standards, however, can become cumbersome and costly.

Have you properly focused your controls? As noted earlier, interdependencies between various tasks, technologies and phases of the production system can be quite significant. If your target of control is too narrow (e.g., "The guy just isn't willing to make a reasonable effort."), you may be missing a more complex situation and find that your remedies don't really work.

Have you determined proper intervals between assessments? You need to find a happy medium in this area. It might seem ideal to continually monitor fulfillment of the plan--and information technologies do, in fact, enable you to do this in some situations. The cost of frequent measurements can, nevertheless, become prohibitive.

Should you reward or punish to correct discrepancies? Both of these usually are used. However, overuse of punishment can lead to negative feelings and, eventually, failure to meet goals. Additionally, negative controls--punishment systems--require much more time to administer. This is because you constantly need to watch for deviations from desired behaviors if you are to catch and effectively punish offenders. A reward system, on the other hand, links appropriate actions to rewards, increasing the likelihood that you will observe positive contributions without the need for careful or frequent monitoring of day-to-day activities.

As you can see, control, like implementation, cannot be treated as an afterthought if you are to be successful in whatever strategy you choose. The standards are determined early in the strategic planning process as you set clear operative goals. Effective measurement and correction systems are crucial if you hope to encourage consistent performance that will lead to the realization of your strategic goals.

10. Summary

Strategic planning has become more important to business managers because technology and competition have made the business environment less stable and less predictable. If you are to survive and prosper, you should take the time to identify the niches in which you are most likely to succeed and to identify the resource demands that must be met. In larger businesses the steps outlined in this guide may be carried out by teams of experts or may involve the interplay of ideas among hundreds, even thousands, of managers. These guidelines are equally applicable to the entrepreneur sitting down with several key employees to discuss what can be achieved in the next two to three years, and what it will cost. The amount of time spent on each step and the resources devoted to this process will vary greatly from business to business, but it is vital to understand and employ these steps. The questions in the self-assessment questionnaire below will help you recall the steps involved in developing a strategic plan.

Self-Assessment Questionnaire

Have you developed a clear sense of direction or mission?

Have you clearly defined the nature of your business?

Do you have a clear philosophy for conducting your business affairs?

Are your business goals obtainable?

Are your objectives logically related in a hierarchy that will lead to goal achievement?

Are your objectives clear, measurable and tied to goal achievement?

Do you periodically reevaluate your objectives to be sure they have not grown obsolete?

Have you developed a logical and planned approach for collecting data on your environment?

Are data stored or filed in ways that allow easy retrieval of useful information?

Are reports produced that are seldom or never used?

Do you periodically review your information system to make certain it is useful and up-to-date?

Can you list four or five key strengths of your business?

Are you aware of key weaknesses in your business?

In developing your final strategy, did you consider three or four possible alternatives?

Are you involving your employees in planning decisions?

Did you take time to communicate the final plan to employees and deal with their concerns?

Is your timetable for implementation of the plan realistic?

Have you scheduled definite checkpoints for assessing progress toward goals?

Have you developed effective ways of measuring progress?

11. A System For Applying The Strategic Plan in Your Business

You can use the system described in this chapter to implement your strategic plan.

Many authorities on business management identify five functions of management:

planning,

organizing,

directing,

controlling, and

coordinating.

Management Business planning and controlling functions often get less attention from owner-managers of businesses than they should. One way to strengthen both of these functions is through effective goal setting.

Long range goals for sales, profits, competitive position, development of people, and industrial relations must be established. Then, goals are set for the current year which will lead towards the accomplishment of the long range goals.

This guide presents Management by Objectives to the owner-manager of a company for use in this type of management business planning and goal setting. MBO includes goal setting by all managers down to the first level of supervision. Their goals are tied to those of the company.

Traditionally, people have worked according to job descriptions that list the activities of the job. The Management by Objectives (MBO) approach, on the other hand, stresses results.

Let's look at an example. Suppose that you have a credit manager and that his or her job description simply says that the credit manager supervises the credit operations of the company. The activities of the credit manager are then listed. Under MBO, the credit manager could have five or six goals covering important aspects of the work. One goal might be to increase credit sales enough to support a 15 percent increase in sales.

The traditional job description for a personnel specialist might include language about conducting the recruiting program for your company. Under MBO, the specialist's work might be covered in five or six goals - one which could be "recruit five new employees in specified categories by July 1."

Thus, MBO looks for results, not activities. With MBO, you view the job in terms of what it should achieve. Activity is never the essential element. It is merely an intermediate step leading to the desired result.

What Business Am I In?

In making long range plans, the first question you ought to think about is "what business am I in?" Is the definition you have of your business is right for today's market?

Are there emerging customer needs that will require a changed definition of your business next year?

For example, one owner-manager's business was making metal trash cans. When sales began to fall off, the owner was forced to reexamine the business. To regain lost sales and continue to grow the owner redefined the product as metal containers and developed a marketing plan for that product.

How you view your business will provide the framework for your planning with respect to markets, product development, buildings and equipment, financial needs, and staff size.

Your long range objectives for your business will be the cornerstone in the MBO program for your company. At a minimum, they must be clearly communicated to your managers; however, for a truly vital program your managers should have a part in formulating these long range goals. Your managers will base their short range goals on these objectives. If they have had a role in establishing the long range objectives, they will be more committed to achieving them.

The Complete MBO Program

Management by Objectives may be used in all kinds of organizations. But not everyone has had the same degree of success in using this concept. From examining those MBO programs that failed, it is clear that the programs were incomplete.

The minimum requirements for an MBO program are:

Each manager's job includes five to ten goals expressed in specific, measurable terms.

Each manager reporting to you proposes his or her goals to you in writing. When you both agree on each goal, a final written statement of the goal is prepared.

Each goal consists of the statement of the goal, how it will be measured, and the work steps necessary to complete it.

Results are systematically determine at regular intervals (at least quarterly) and compared with the goals.

When progress towards goals is not in accordance with your plans, problems are identified and corrective action is taken.

Goals at each level of management are related to the level above and the level below.

Goal Setting

Goals for each of your managers are the crucial element in any MBO system. Goals at middle level of management must be consistent with those at top levels. Goals of first line supervisors must relate to those at middle levels. Goals prepared by the manager responsible for certain steps in a large processing operation must tie in with those of managers responsible for other steps in the processing. And all goals must relate to and support your long range objectives for the company.

When all these goals are consistent, then an MBO system will be developed. Until then, there will be many like the middle manager of a research and development company who exclaimed in a seminar, "How can I set my goals when I don't know where top management wants to go?"

Each manager will probably find between five and eight goals enough to cover those aspects of the job crucial to successful performance. These are the elements which you will use to judge his or her performance. Of course, other duties which do not fall into the above goals should not be neglected. But they are of secondary importance.

When you first start your MBO program, your managers will undergo a learning period. They must learn how to prepare a goal which will make them stretch but is not beyond their capabilities. They must learn to develop ways to effectively measure real problems which threaten the achievement of the goals and then take steps to cope with the problems.

During this learning period, your managers should first set a few goals. Then as they learn how to develop and achieve goals, the coverage and number of goals can be extended.

The Miniature Work Plan

Your managers may find the miniature work plan useful. On this work plan the manager can show each of the major work steps (sub-goals) necessary to reach the goal. Then, if each work step is performed by the indicated date, the goal will be reached when the last work step is completed.

You may also use this form to discuss goals with your manager. By looking at this form, you can see not only the goal but also the plan for reaching that goal. This will allow you to ask questions about the work steps and anticipated problems, as well as to question how the goal will be measured. By pointing out the relationship between the manager's goal and your goal, you'll be helping each of your managers to understand how his/her goals relate to those of the company.

A Manager's Goal

Instructions for Completing Form

Management by Objectives provides for the establishment of four to ten goals by each manager. You should set up goals in each of several important areas in your job. You might try to establish at least one in each of these categories: Regular, Problem Solving, Innovative, and Development. By following this approach you will be more likely to see the full range of possibilities open to you through goal setting.

Develop each goal as a miniature work plan. The steps that follow will result in goals which are complete and useful to both you and your boss.

Goal (Be specific and concise)

_____

Measurement (The bench mark that tells you that you have achieved the goal, should be expressed in quantitative terms)

_____

Problems Anticipated

_____

_____

Work Steps (List three or four most essential steps, give completion dates for each)

_____

_____

_____

Superior's Goal (Give goal at next higher level to which your goal relates).

_____

_____

Whenever a problem is listed on the work plan, the manager should include a work step to deal with it. For example, suppose the head of your supply department set a goal to deliver all packages within one day of when they were received. He thought he might have difficulty in getting his people to follow the new procedures. So, he included a work step to teach these procedures before the new program went into effect.

Kinds of Goals

When your managers begin to set their goals, they may want to know what areas are suitable for goal setting. What are the really important aspects of their jobs rather than that part which is most visible to them? How can they be sure that their program is balanced for the long haul, rather than just reacting to immediate, pressing problems? How can they set goals which are most likely to help them control their jobs?

It might be useful for them to have a classification of goals that suggests areas of opportunity. Generally, each manager should have between five and eight goals. One or two goals in each of these areas should be helpful:

1. Regular work goals.

2. Problem solving goals.

3. Innovative goals.

4. Development goals.

Regular work refers to those activities which make up the major part of the manager's responsibilities. The head of production would be primarily concerned with the amount, quality, and efficiency of production. The head of marketing would be primarily concerned with developing and conducting the market research and sales programs. Each manager should be able to find opportunities to operate more efficiently, to improve the quality of the product or service, and to expand the total amount produced or marketed.

Problem solving goals will give your managers an opportunity to define their major problems. There is no danger of anyone ever running out of problems. New problems or new versions of old problems always seem to replace those overcome.

Innovative goals may be viewed the same way. A goal for innovation may apply to an actual problem. But, some innovation may not deal with a problem. For example, the head of building management sets a goal to invigorate the employee suggestion program by putting five suggestions into effect during the next four months. There was no specific to be solved, the manager was just trying to do the best job possible.

The development goal recognizes how important the development of your employees is to your business. Your managers can be encouraged to develop their people just as they are to produce more effectively. Every manager must be to some extent a teacher and a coach; each manager must plan for the employees' continued growth in both technical area and in working together effectively.

By asking your managers to set at least one goal in the four areas listed above, you may open their eyes to possibilities they had not seen before. the goal setting process can be a very useful educational step, even for those who are primarily specialists.

Progress Reports

An MBO program without provision for regular reports on progress is worthless. That is why some articles and books on MBO call the concept MBO/R. The "R" refers to results. Nothing is accomplished by setting goals or objectives unless the program calls for a regular review of progress towards results.

A large organization issued nearly 100 pages of goals prepared by many of its managers. Most of the goals were well developed. The document was very impressive. But there was absolutely no provision for a reporting system of any kind. It is easy to imagine the reaction of those who set goals for the first year when they were asked the following year to draw up new goals.

A monthly or quarterly review of progress towards goals will help you determine where progress is below expectations. For example, suppose that one of your goals calls for a reduction of overtime by 50 percent this year, and the first quarter reduction is only 15 percent. A special effort must be exerted in the succeeding quarters to regain the lost ground or the goal will not be achieved by the end of the year. When progress is below expectations, the problem or problems holding back progress should be identified and assigned to someone, usually the manager, for resolution. Make these assignments part of the company MBO files so that responsibility for correcting the problem areas cannot be evaded.

Performance Evaluation

You will have to evaluate the performance of every person working for you in some way, either formally or informally. When your managers are working to achieve a full set of five to eight goals, their ability to get results on each goal can be a good, objective measure of performance.

Traditional performance evaluation systems have been strongly criticized because they deal with subjective matters such as leadership qualities, rather than the more objective measure of results. Evaluating performance by MBO, while objective, is a complex task, which must be undertaken with care by someone who fully understands MBO. Failure to reach goals can be a result of setting the wrong objectives in the first place, the existence of organizational restrictions not taken into account, inadequate or improper measures of goal achievement, personal failure, or a combination of factors.

Installing MBO

When installing an MBO program, many owner-managers have found it best to start their jobs by asking their managers to define their jobs. What are their major responsibilities? Then, for each responsibility, the manager and the boss decide how they will measure performance in terms of results.

The result of this exercise may surprise you. Often managers and their bosses do not even agree on the manager's major responsibilities. Also, you may find that no one is performing some of the functions that you consider important.

As the owner-manager, you must appreciate what the system will do. You have to show interest in the concept from the beginning. You have to set the example for your subordinate managers, if the MBO system is to be a success

The education of your managers may be a formidable task. They have probably thought in terms of specific functions - managing a sales department, directing a credit office - rather than in terms of goals which contribute to the organization.

It might be best to start with a seminar of six to nine hours in a classroom. This ought to be enough to introduce MBO to the managers who will be setting goals. Either you or a consultant might conduct the seminar. (If you choose a consultant, be sure that you are there for the entire seminar).

Provide enough time so that your managers can express their doubts, reservations or opposition to MBO. It is best to get their feelings out into the open as soon as possible. Other participants can help them deal with their concerns.

A very useful part of such a seminar is the preparation of an actual goal by each participant. In small group sessions, your mangers can help each other by reviewing work plans and offering suggestions to improve each others plans.

Working with goal setting, periodic review of goals, and other aspects of MBO will be a learning experience for most managers. If they set annual goals, it may take three to four years before good results from this system of managing appear. MBO may look simple on the surface, but it requires experience and skill to make it work effectively.

Threats to the MBO System

Not all MBO programs are successful. Some of the leading reasons why past programs failed to reach their potential are:

1. Top management did not get involved.

2. Corporate objectives were inadequate.

3. MBO was installed as a crash program.

4. It was difficult to learn the system because the nature of MBO was not taught.

It is hard to get people to think in terms of results rather than activities relating to their work. However, it can be done. The sequence of steps one owner-manager uses may not work for another. It is often an individual matter. Results are what count.

If you feel that you are ready to introduce MBO to your company, why not set this as a goal for yourself. Turn back and follow through the work plan. List your goal, measurement, anticipated problems, and the work steps necessary to get your company managing by objectives.

12. Creating a Business Environment that Supports Growth

Manage a business effectively, manage staff effectively, is the key to the establishment and growth of the business. The key to successful management is to examine the marketplace environment and create employment and profit opportunities that provide the potential growth and financial viability of the business. Despite the importance of management, this area is often misunderstood and poorly implemented, primarily because people focus on the output rather than the process of management.

Toward the end of the 1980s, business managers became absorbed in improving product quality, sometimes ignoring their role vis-a-vis personnel. The focus was on reducing costs and increasing output, while ignoring the long-term benefits of motivating personnel. This shortsighted view tended to increase profits in the short term, but created a dysfunctional long-term business environment.

Simultaneously with the increase in concern about quality, entrepreneurship attracted the attention of business. A sudden wave of successful entrepreneurs seemed to render earlier management concepts obsolete. The popular press focused on the new cult heroes Steve Jobs and Steve Wozniack (creators and developers of the Apple Computer) while ignoring the marketing and organizing talents of Mike Markula, the executive responsible for Apple's business plan. The story of two guys selling their Volkswagen bus to build the first Apple computer was more romantic than that of the organizational genius that enabled Apple to develop, market and ship its products while rapidly becoming a major corporation.

In large businesses, effective manage business skills requires planning. Planning is essential for developing a firm's potential. However, many small businesses do not recognize the need for long-range plans, because the small number of people involved in operating the business implies equal responsibility in the planning and decision-making processes. Nevertheless, the need for planning is as important in a small business as it is in a large one.

This guide focuses on the importance of good management practices. Specifically, it addresses the responsibilities of managing the external and internal environments.

MANAGING THE EXTERNAL ENVIRONMENT

Three decades ago, Alvin Toffler suggested that the vision of the citizen in the tight grip of an omnipotent bureaucracy would be replaced by an organizational structure of ad-hocracy. The traditional business organization implied a social contract between employees and employers. By adhering to a fixed set of obligations and sharply defined roles and responsibilities, employees received a predefined set of rewards.

The organizational structure that Toffler predicted in 1970 became the norm 20 years later, and with it came changed concepts of authority. As organizations became more transitory, the authority of the organization and firm was replaced by the authority of the individual manager. This entrepreneurial management model is now being replicated throughout society. As a result, the individual business owner must internalize ever increasing organizational functions.

Another change in today's business environment is dealing with government agencies. Their effect on the conduct of business most recently appears to have increased. As industries fail to achieve high levels of ethical behavior or individual businesses exhibit specific lapses, the government rushes in to fill the breach with its regulations.

MANAGING THE INTERNAL ENVIRONMENT

HUMAN RESOURCE ISSUES

Ensuring Open Communications

Effective communications play an integral role in managing and operating any successful business. With open communications changes and their effects on the organization are quickly shared. Your firm then has the time and skills needed to respond to changes and take advantage of evolving opportunities.

The following checklist addressing how you would respond to an employee's suggestion provides an assessment of the communication process in your business. Place a check next to the statements that are commonly heard in your business.

Statement

Face facts it's unrealistic. -----

Who else has done it? -----

It's not your problem. -----

Fill out form XX/xx revised. -----

It won't work. -----

Bring it to the committee. -----

We don't have the time. -----

We tried it before and it failed. -----

You think what? You're joking! -----

Everybody knows that that's foolish. -----

We can't afford to think about it. -----

Don't you have better things to do? -----

Are you some kind of a radical? -----

We're too small/big for that. -----

Impossible; our main product line would be obsolete. -----

The boss would never consider it. -----

It's contrary to company policy. -----

Carefully consider any statements that you have checked. This may indicate that management is inflexible and unresponsive to employee suggestions. Management that is unable to respond immediately to changes in the market signals an inflexible unstable firm. In the rapidly changing business environment such management can mean eventual failure for your business. If you haven't developed such a checklist do so. It will help you determine if and where adjustments are needed in your management staff.

Balancing Schedules Stress and Personnel

Without organization and good management the compressed time schedules associated with modern business can cause stress and make extraordinary demands on people. An effective management structure can reduce stress and channel the productive capacity of employees into business growth and profits.

Setting Duties Tasks and Responsibilities

An organization is characterized by the nature and determination of employees' duties tasks and responsibilities. While many organizations use different methods for determining these it is essential that they be clearly defined.

The core of any organization is its people and their functions. Duties tasks and responsibilities often evolve in an ad hoc manner. A typical firm starts with a few people often one performing all duties. As the firm grows others are hired to fill specific roles often on a functional basis. Roles that were handled by consultants and specialists outside the firm now are handled internally. As new needs emerge new roles are developed.

Just as an emerging business develops an accounting system it should also develop a human resource system. For instance the following employee information should be available and checked for accuracy at least once each year.

- Name

- Address

- Nationality (immigration status)

- Marital status and dependents

- Hire date

- Company job history:

- Title and code

- Performance

- Location

- Salary rate and history

- Education including degrees

- Specialty training

- Transcripts as appropriate

- Pre-employment work experience:

- Key responsibilities and levels

- Professional licenses or certificates

- Professional publication and speaking engagements

- Teaching experience

- Language abilities:

- Reading

- Writing

- Speaking

- Leadership evidence:

- Company

- Civic

- Other

- Relocation preferences and limitations

- Travel experience and preferences

- Career goals

Review your personnel files periodically to ensure that the information is correct and current. Implement a system that will make updating personnel files a fairly simple routine yet confidential process.

Business Team

The apex of an effective organization lies in developing the business team. Such a team involves delegating authority and increasing productivity.

Assess the effectiveness of your business team with the following checklist:

The leader of the team is respected by the members. -----

The abilities of all team members are respected. -----

A team spirit is evident through activities. -----

Individual members compensate for weaknesses in each other. -----

Jokes are not disparaging. -----

A genuine feeling of being part of the best is exuded. -----

The work area is self-delineated and reflects a spirit. -----

Mistakes result in corrective action not retribution. -----

Each member understands the importance of his or her contribution. -----

The team can explore new areas of activity. -----

Security of employment is evident. -----

Controlling Conflict

Another key to successful management lies in controlling conflict. Conflict cannot be eliminated from either the business or the interpersonal activities of the enterprise. A measure of the organization's success is the degree to which conflict can be exposed and the energies associated with it channeled to develop the firm. Although establishing policies and procedures represents the tangible aspect of organization and management the mechanisms to tolerate and embody challenges to the established operation serve as the real essence of a firm that will survive and prosper.

Structural Issues

Organization

The effectiveness of a particular organizational form depends on a variety of internal and external events for example:

Competitors (number or activity)

Technology (internal or external)

Regulatory environment

Customer characteristics

Supplier characteristics

Economic environment

Key employees

Growth

Strategy (including new products and markets)

Even though you may discover that certain events are affecting your business be careful not to change the organizational structure of your firm without discussing it with your management team. Employees generally can accomplish goals despite organizational structures imposed by management. Because restructuring involves spending a lot of time learning new rules implementing a new organizational structure is costly.

Structure

The essence of a successful organization can be more simply summarized than implemented. The following checklist can help you determine measures to ensure your management structure is adequate. Check the entries that apply to your firm and also find out what measures your company needs to take to improve its management structure.

Key market and customers are understood. -----

Technology is mastered. -----

Key objectives are articulated and shared. -----

Major functions are identified and staffed. -----

A hierarchy of relationships is established. -----

A business team is in place and functioning. -----

Measurable results are well above industry standards. -----

Employees are the best source of new hires. -----

Policy and Procedural Issues

Authority

The central element of organizational management is authority. Through authority your firm develops the structure necessary to achieve its objectives.

A. L. Stinchcombe summarized the role of authority succinctly when he stated any administrative system that decides on the use of resources is also a system of authority directing the activities of people.

The authority that once was conferred by either owning a small business or having a position in the bureaucracy of a larger firm has been replaced by technical competence (including that of forming and running the business). Forces external to your business may emphasize the elements of granted versus earned authority. Once the owner-manager controlled the entire business but suppliers customers unions and the government have severely limited the ability of the business owner-manager to take independent action.

A primary component of authority is the exercise of control within the organization. A thorough system of controls ensures the firm's operation and provides a mechanism for imposing authority. Internal controls include the provision that authority be delegated and circumscribed; examples of these provisions follow. Place a check by the provisions that apply to your firm. Consider implementing controls over areas that you have not checked.

Approval for disbursements of cash and regular accounting. -----

Reconciliation of bank statements. -----

Periodic count and reconciliation of inventory records. -----

Approval of pricing policies and exemptions. -----

Approval of credit policies and exemptions. -----

Review of expense and commission accounts. -----

Approval of purchasing and receiving policies. -----

Review of payments to vendors and employees. -----

Approval of signature authorities for payments. -----

Review of policies. -----

Delegation is a key to the effective exercise of authority in your business. By delegating limited authority to accomplish specific tasks the talents of employees in the organization can be used to upgrade the skills and experience of the manager. The following checklist enables you to determine if you are taking advantage of opportunities to delegate authority.

Is your time consumed by daily chores? -----

Do you have time for the following:

- Training and development of subordinates? -----

- Planning? -----

- Coordinating and controlling work of subordinates? -----

- Visiting customers and subordinates regularly? -----

- Remaining involved in new product development? -----

- Visiting branch locations regularly? -----

- Attending business meetings outside your business? -----

- Participating in civic affairs? -----

Is no one on your staff as good as you are? -----

To effectively delegate responsibility and authority in your organization you must:

Accept the power of delegation.

Know the capabilities of subordinates.

Ensure that specific training is available.

Select specific responsibilities to be delegated.

Clearly define the extent and limits of delegation.

Match each with necessary authority.

Provide periodic monitoring and interest.

Restrain the impulse to insist on how to do something.

Remember there are many ways to accomplish a specific objective.

Assess results and provide appropriate feedback.

Praise and criticize.

The skills and abilities of each level of authority can be increased by effectively delegating authority throughout any organization.

Operating Reports

Operating reports form the organizational basis of your business. Such reports mirror the organization its structure and function. They define key relationships between employees and can either minimize or increase organizational stress.

For many businesses the following reports form the basis for analyzing the specific areas of a business (the frequency of each report depends on the nature size and organization of your business). Check the reports your firm currently generates.

Consider creating reporting systems where they are lacking.

Case reports (daily, weekly, monthly) -----

New orders and backlog (weekly, monthly) -----

Shipments/sales (weekly, monthly) -----

Employment (monthly) -----

Inventory out of stock (weekly, monthly) -----

Product quality (weekly, monthly) -----

Accounts receivable aging accounts (monthly) -----

Weekly overdue accounts -----

Returns and allowances (monthly) -----

Production (weekly, monthly) -----

Reporting must be kept current to allow for timely identification and correction of problems before serious damage to the organization occurs.

Too much reporting as well as inappropriate reporting can be as destructive as too little reporting. For instance the CEO of a major industrial firm who receives daily production and inventory reports by model can lose his or her ability to maintain an overall perspective. Thus operating managers must attempt to identify and solve local problems and take advantage of local opportunities within their own authority. Inappropriate reporting compromises management's ability to leverage individual skills and abilities.

Operating reports not only provide essential data that enable management to accomplish its objectives they also focus staff's attention on the organization's goals. If reporting is not taken seriously employees may deal with customers suppliers and each other in a similarly trivial manner.

To avoid inappropriate reporting review reporting policies annually to ensure that reports are appropriate and contain the information needed to make sound management decisions.

Conclusion

Successful management is founded on the mastery of a myriad of details. While management schools teach the importance of focusing attention on major issues affecting the business practical managers realize the major issues are the variety of small aspects that form the business. In an increasingly structured society inattention to even one minor detail can result in significant disruption of the business or even its failure.

Checklist For An Effective Organization

The following checklist will help you identify and determine the effectiveness of the management and organizational structure of the firm. If you answer yes to most of the following questions you are effectively managing your firm. A no answer indicates that you need to focus on this management issue.

yes / no

Are responsibilities clear and matched by authority? -----

Is your business structure clear yet flexible? -----

Are communications focused on finding solutions rather than placing blame? -----

Do people have the information and resources necessary to do an excellent job? -----

Do you and your employees care about the business? -----

Does staff come in early and stay late on their own initiative? -----

Are mechanisms for conflict resolution working? -----

Is disorder minimized and channeled? -----

Can people joke with and about each other and you? -----

Does a corporate plan spell out the firm's vision? -----

Do employees pitch in unasked during a crisis? -----

Do customers and suppliers prefer to do business with you?

13. How to Ensure That Your Business is On The Right Path

Making a profit is the most important - some might say the only - objective of a business. Profit measures success. It can be defined simply: Revenues - Expenses = Profit. So, to increase profits you must raise revenues, lower expenses, or both. To make improvements you must know what's really going on financially at all times. You have to watch every financial event without any kind of optimistic filter.

This financial management analysis Guide is a series of questions with comments to help you analyze your profits, their sufficiency and trend, the contribution of each of your product lines or services to them, and to help you determine if you have the kind of record system you need. The questions and comments are not meant to be definitive presentations on the subjects. They are meant to point to areas where further study might be - well - profitable.

Are You making A Profit?

Financial Analysis of Revenues and Expenses

Since profit is revenues less expenses, to determine what your profit is you must first identify all revenues and expenses for the period under study.

1. Have you chosen an appropriate period for profit determination?

For accounting purposes firms generally use a twelve month period, such as January 1 to December 31 or July 1 to June 30. The accounting year you select doesn't have to be a calendar year (January to December); a seasonal business, for example, might close its year after the end of the season. The selection depends upon the nature of your business, your personal preference, or possible tax considerations.

2. Have you determined your total revenues for the accounting period?

In order to answer this question, consider the following questions:

What is the amount of gross revenue from sales of your goods or service? (Gross Sales)

What is the amount of goods returned by your customers and credited? (Returns and Rejects)

What is the amount of discounts given to your customers and employees? (Discounts)

What is the amount of net sales from goods and services? **(Net Sales =** Gross Sales - Returns and Rejects + Discounts))

What is the amount of income from other sources, such as interest on bank deposits, dividends from securities, rent on property leased to others? (Non-operating Income)

What is the amount of total revenue? (Total Revenue = Net Sales + Non-operating Income)

3. Do you know what your total expenses are?

Expenses are the cost of goods sold and services used in the process of selling goods or services. Some common expenses for all businesses are:

Cost of goods sold (Cost of Goods Sold = Beginning Inventory + Purchases - Ending Inventory)

Wages and salaries (Don't forget to include your own- at the actual rate - you'd have to pay someone else to do your job.)

Rent

Utilities (electricity, gas telephone, water, etc.)

Delivery expenses

Insurance

Advertising and promotional costs

Maintenance and upkeep

Depreciation (Here you need to make sure your depreciation policies are realistic and that all depreciable items are included)

Taxes and licenses

Interest

Bad debts

Professional assistance (accountant, attorney, etc.)

There are of course, many other types of expenses, but the point is that every expense must be recorded and deducted from your revenues before you know what your profit is. Understanding your expenses is the first step toward controlling them and increasing your profit.

Financial Ratios

A financial ratio is an expression on the relationship between two items selected from the income statement or the balance sheet. Ratio analysis helps you evaluate the weak and strong points in your financial and managerial performance.

4. Do you know your current ratio?

The current ratio (current assets divided by current debts) is a measure of the cash or near cash position (liquidity) of the firm. It tells you if you have enough cash to pay your firm's current creditors. The higher the ratio, the more liquid the firm's position is and, hence, the higher the credibility of the firm. Cash, receivables, marketable securities, and inventory are current assets. Naturally you need to be realistic in valuing receivable and inventory for a true picture of your liquidity, since some debts may be un-collectable and some stock obsolete. Current liabilities are those which must be paid in one year.

5. Do you know your quick ratio?

Quick assets are current assets minus inventory. The quick ratio (or acid-test ratio) is found by dividing quick assets by current liabilities. The purpose, again, is to test the firm's ability to meet its current obligations. This test doesn't include inventory to make it a stiffer test of the company's liquidity. It tells you if the business could meet its current obligations with quickly convertible assets should sales revenue suddenly cease.

6. Do you know your total debt to net worth ratio?

This ratio (the result of total debt divided by net worth then multiplied by 100) is a measure of how company can meet its total obligation from equity. The lower the ratio, the higher the proportion of equity relative to debt and the better the firm's credit rating will be.

7. Do you know your average collection period?

You find this ratio by dividing accounts receivable by daily credit sales. (Daily credit sales = annual credit sales divided by 360.) This ratio tells you the length of time it takes the firm to get its cash after making a sale on credit. The shorter this period the quicker the cash flow is. A longer than normal period may mean overdue and un-collectible bills. If you extend credit for a specific period (say, 30 days), this ratio should be very close to the same number of day. If it's much longer than the established period, you may need to alter your credit policies. It's wise to develop an aging schedule to gauge the trend of collections (without adequate financing charges) hurt your profit, since you could be doing something much more useful with your money, such as taking advantage of discounts on your own payables.

8. Do you know your ratio of net sales to total assets?

This ratio (net sales divided by total assets) measures the efficiency with which you are using your assets. A higher than normal ratio indicates that the firm is able to generate sales from its assets faster (and better) than the average concern.

9. Do you know your operating profit to net sales ratio?

This ratio (the result of dividing operating profit by net sales and multiplying by 100) is most often used to determine the profit position relative to sales. A higher than normal ratio indicates that your sales are good, that your expenses are low, or both. Interest income and interest expense should not be included in calculating this ratio.

10. Do you know your net profit to total assets ratio?

This ratio (found by multiplying by 100 the result of dividing net profit by total assets) is often called return on investment or ROI. It focuses on the profitability of the overall operation of the firm. Thus, it allows management to measure the effects of its policies on the firm's profitability. The ROI is the single most important measure of a firm's financial position. You might say it's the bottom line for the bottom line.

11. Do you know your net profit to net worth ratio?

This ratio is found by dividing net profit by net worth and multiplying the result by 100. It provides information on the productivity of the resources the owners have committed to the firm's operations.

All ratios measuring profitability can be computed either before or after taxes, depending on the purpose of the computations. Ratios have limitations. Since the information used to derive ratios is itself based on accounting rules and personal judgments, as well as facts, the ratios cannot be considered absolute indicators of a firm's financial position. Ratios are only one means of assessing the performance of the firm and must be considered in perspective with many other measures. They should be used as a point of departure for further analysis and not as an end in themselves.

Sufficiency Of Profit

The following questions are designed to help you measure the adequacy of the profit your firm is making. Making a profit is only the first step; making enough profit to survive and grow is really what business is all about.

12. Have you compared your profit with your profit goals?

13. Is it possible your goals are too high or too low?

14. Have you compared your present profits (absolute and ratios) with the profits made in the last one to three years?

15. Have you compared your profits (absolute and ratios) with profits made by similar firms in your line?2

DEVELOPING A STRATEGIC PLAN

A number of organizations publish financial ratios for various businesses, among them Dun & Bradstreet. Robert Morris Associates, the Accounting Corporation of America, NCR Corporation, and the Bank of America. Your own trade association may also publish such studies. Remember, these published ratios are only averages. You probably want to be better than average.

Trend Of Profit

16. Have you analyzed the direction your profits have been taking?

The preceding analysis, with all their merits, report on a firm only at a single time in the past. It is not possible to use these isolated moments to indicate the trend of your firm's performance. To do a trend analysis performance indicators (absolute amounts or ratios) should be computed for several time periods (yearly for several years, for example) and the results laid out in columns side by side for easy comparison. You can then evaluate your performance, see the direction it's taking, and make initial forecasts of where it will go.

17. Does your firm sell more than one major product line or provide several distinct services?

If it does, a separate profit and ratio analysis of each should be made:

To show the relative contribution by each product line or service;

To show the relative burden of expenses by each product or service;

To show which items are most profitable, which are less so, and which are losing money; and

To show which are slow and fast moving.

Mix Of Profit

The profit analysis of each major item help you find out the strong and weak areas of your operations. They can help you to make profit-increasing decisions to drop a product line or service or to place particular emphasis behind one or another.

Records

Good records are essential. Without them a firm doesn't know where it's been, where it is, or where it's heading. Keeping records that are accurate, up-to-date, and easy to use is one of the most important functions of the owner-manager, his or her staff, and his or her outside counselors (lawyer, accountant, banker).

Basic Records

18. Do you have a general journal and/or special journals, such as one for cash receipts and disbursements?

A general journal is the basic record of the firm. Every monetary event in the life of the firm is entered in the general journal or in one of the special journals.

19. Do you prepare a sales report or analysis?

(a) Do you have sales goals by product, department, and accounting period (month, quarter, year)?

(b) Are your goals reasonable?

(c) Are you meeting your goals?

If you aren't meeting your goals, try to list the likely reasons on a sheet of paper. Such a study might include areas such as general business climate, competition, pricing, advertising, sales promotion, credit policies, and the like. Once you've identified the apparent causes you can take steps to increase sales (and profits).

Buying and Inventory System

20. Do you have a buying and inventory system?

The buying and inventory systems are two critical areas of a firm's operation that can affect profitability.

21. Do you keep records on the quality, service, price, and promptness of delivery of your sources of supply?

22. Have you analyzed the advantages and disadvantages of:

(a) Buying from several suppliers,

(b) Buying from a minimum number of suppliers?

23. Have you analyzed the advantages and disadvantages of buying through cooperatives or other systems?

24. Do you know:

(a) How long it usually takes to receive each order?

(b) How much inventory cushion (usually called safety stock) to have so you can maintain normal sales while you wait for the order to arrive?

25. Have you ever suffered because you were out of stock?

26. Do you know the optimum order quantity for each item you need?

27. Do you (or can you) take advantage of quantity discounts for large size single purchases?

28. Do you know your costs of ordering inventory and carrying inventory?

The more frequently you buy (smaller quantities per order), the higher your average ordering costs (clerical costs, postage, telephone costs etc.) will be, and the lower the average carrying costs (storage, loss through pilferage, obsolescence, etc.) will be. On the other hand, the larger the quantity per order, the lower the average ordering cost and the higher the carrying costs. A balance should be struck so that the minimum cost overall for ordering and carrying inventory can be achieved.

29. Do you keep records of inventory for each item?

These records should be kept current by making entries whenever items are added to or removed from inventory. Simple records on 3 x 5 or 5 x 7 cards can be used with each item being listed on a separate card. Proper records will show for each item: quantity in stock, quantity on order, date of order, slow or fast seller, and valuations (which are important for taxes and your own analyses.)

Other Financial Records

30. Do you have an accounts payable ledger?

This ledger will show what, whom, and why you owe. Such records should help you make your payments on schedule. Any expense not paid on time could adversely affect your credit, but even more importantly such records should help you take advantage of discounts which can help boost your profits.

31. Do you have an accounts receivable ledger?

This ledger will show who owes money to your firm. It shows how much is owed, how long it has been outstanding and why the money is owed. Overdue accounts could indicate that your credit granting policy needs to be reviewed and that you may not be getting the cash into the firm quickly enough to pay your own bills at the optimum time.

32. Do you have a cash receipts journal?

This journal records the cash received by source, day, and amount.

33. Do you have a cash payments journal?

This journal will be similar to the cash receipts journal but will show cash paid out instead of cash received. The two cash journals can be combined, if convenient.

34. Do you prepare an income (profit and loss or P&L) statement and a balance sheet?

These are statements about the condition of your firm at a specific time and show the income, expenses, assets, and liabilities of the firm. They are absolutely essential.

35. Do you prepare a budget?

You could think of a budget as a "record in advance," projecting "future" inflows and outflows for your business. A budget is usually prepared for a single year, generally to correspond with the accounting year. It is then, however broken down into quarterly and monthly projections.

There are different kinds of budget: cash,

production, sales, etc. A cash budget, for example, will show the estimate of sales and expenses for a particular period of time. The cash budget forces the firm to think ahead by estimating its income and expenses. Once reasonable projections are made for every important product line or department, the owner-manager has set targets for employees to meet for sales and expenses. You must plan to assure a profit. And you must prepare a budget to plan.

* * * *

Appendix: Special Free Bonuses

You can access your free bonuses here:

https://www.bizmove.com/bizgifts.htm

Here's what you get:

#1 How to Be a Good Manager and Leader; 120 Tips to improve your Leadership Skills (Leadership Video Guide).

Learn how to improve your leadership skills and become a better manager and leader. Here's how to be the boss people want to give 200 percent for. In this video you'll discover 120 powerful tips and strategies to motivate and inspire your people to bring out the best in them.

#2 Small Business Management: Essential Ingredients for Success (eBook Guide)

Discover scores of business management tricks, secrets and shortcuts. This Ebook guide does far more than impart knowledge - it inspires action.

#3 How to Manage Yourself for Success; 90 Tips to Better Manage Yourself and Your Time (Self Management Video Guide)

You are responsible for everything that happens in your life. Learn to accept total responsibility for yourself. If you don't manage yourself, then you are letting others have control of your life. In this video you'll discover 90 powerful tips and strategies to better manage yourself for success.

#4 80 Best Inspirational Quotes for Success (Motivational Video Guide)

For this video we scanned thousands of motivational and inspirational quotes to bring you this collection of the best 80 motivational quotes for success in life.

#5 Top 10 Habits to Adopt From Highly Successful People (Self Growth Video Guide)

In this video you'll discover the top 10 habits of highly successful people that you can adopt and achieve success in your life.

#6 Personal Branding: How to Make a Killer First Impression (Self Promotion Video Guide)

This video deals with personal branding. While promoting your personal brand, you'll discover in this video the ten most effective things you can do to make the best first impression possible.

#7 How to Advance Your Career 10 Times Faster (Career Advancement Video Guide)

The most important thing to remember about your

career today is that you need to be responsible for your own future. In this video you'll discover 10 powerful strategies to advance your career faster.

#8 How to Get Success in Life; 10 Strategies to Attract the Life You Want (Self Actualization Video Guide)

To have more, we must be more of who we are. The secret is in the doing; none of it matters until we do something about it. In this video you'll discover 10 powerful strategies to attract the life you want.

#9 A Comprehensive Package of Business Tools

Here's a collection featuring dozens of business related templates, worksheets, forms, and plans; covering finance, starting a business, marketing, business planning, sales, and general management.

#10 People Management Skills: How to Deal with Difficult Employees (Managing People Video Guide)

Problem behavior on the part of employees can erupt for a variety of reasons. In this video you'll discover the top ten ideas for dealing with difficult employees.

www.ingramcontent.com/pod-product-compliance
Lightning Source LLC
Chambersburg PA
CBHW070807220526
45466CB00002B/580